Garfield's
Guide
To
CREATURES
(GREAT & SMALL)

JIM DAVIS

RAVETTE PUBLISHING

This edition first published by Ravette Publishing Limited 1999.

Printed and bound for Ravette Publishing Limited,
Unit 3, Tristar Centre
Star Road, Partridge Green
West Sussex RH13 8RA

Printed in Slovenija by Mladinska Knjiga in arrangement with Midas Printing UK

ISBN: 1 85304 998 0

© 1991 PAWS, INC.

WAH-HA! HA! HA!

BOY, HAIRCUTS ARE DECEIVING

JIM DAVIS 4-2

JIM DAVIS 4-19
© 1991 PAWS, INC.

WHAT MICE?

BEWARE OF DOG

AH, WINTER... THE SNOWFLAKES GENTLY FALLING...

THE HILLS BLANKETED IN WHITE...

THE CAT'S FACE FROZEN IN THE BIRDBATH

JUST GET THE ICE PICK

THIS HAS GONE TOO FAR!

JIM DAViS 10-27

HEY LOOK! A FLEA COLLAR!

HA HA HA HAAA!

HEY, CAT! WE SPIT ON YOUR FLEA COLLAR!

YEAH!

PTOOEY! PTOOEY! PTOOEY!

WE DANCE ON YOUR FLEA COLLAR!

YEE HAA!

YEEES, IT'S TIME TO REPLACE THE OL' FLEA COLLAR

JIM DAViS 11-24

I FIND YOUR PRESENCE UNPLEASANT

YOU POSSESS MANY SHORTCOMINGS ALSO

JIM DAVIS 11-5

NO ONE IS PERFECT

LET'S GO BACK TO BARK AND HISS

MONDAY, I'M NOT AFRAID OF YOU!

JIM DAVIS 11-18

IN FACT, I LAUGH IN YOUR FACE!

HA! HA! HA! HA! HA!

ZZZZZZZ

© 1996 PAWS, INC./Distributed by Universal Press Syndicate

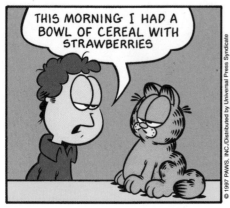